JB Andrew

MUSTANG MAGIC

True HORSE Stories

JB Andrew

MUSTANG MAGIC

BY JUDY ANDREKSON

Illustrations by David Parkins

Tundra Books

Text copyright © 2008 by Judy Andrekson
Illustrations copyright © 2008 by David Parkins

Published in Canada by Tundra Books,
75 Sherbourne Street, Toronto, Ontario M5A 2P9

Published in the United States by Tundra Books of Northern New York,
P.O. Box 1030, Plattsburgh, New York 12901

Library of Congress Control Number: 2007927386

Library and Archives Canada Cataloguing in Publication

Andrekson, Judy
JB Andrew : mustang magic / Judy Andrekson.

(True horse stories)
ISBN 978-0-88776-837-8

1. JB Andrew (Horse)–Juvenile literature. 2. Mustang–Juvenile literature.
3. Wild horses–Juvenile literature. 4. Dressage–Juvenile literature.
I. Title. II. Series.

SF295.565.J3A54 2008   j798.2'30929   C2007-902716-4

We acknowledge the financial support of the Government of Canada
through the Book Publishing Industry Development Program (BPIDP)
and that of the Government of Ontario through the Ontario Media
Development Corporation's Ontario Book Initiative. We further acknowledge
the support of the Canada Council for the Arts and the Ontario Arts Council for
our publishing program.

ONTARIO ARTS COUNCIL
CONSEIL DES ARTS DE L'ONTARIO

Design: Terri Nimmo

Printed and bound in Canada

This book is printed on acid-free paper that is 100% recycled,
ancient-forest friendly (40% post-consumer recycled).

1 2 3 4 5 6   13 12 11 10 09 08

In memory of Louella – a wonderful friend and horsewoman
and for
my gentle sister, Janet, and my long-time best friend, Janice.

Acknowledgments

I would like to extend my deepest gratitude to the special people who assisted me with this story.

Lona Kossner, Debbie Collins, and Glenna Eckel from the Bureau of Land Management were incredibly helpful during my early research, helping me locate Kelly O'Leary, teaching me about the herd Andy came from and the area in which he lived before capture, and about the land management practices of that area. Your help is so greatly appreciated. Thank you.

Ginger Scott, thank you so much for your input. The love and devotion you had (and still have) for this special horse came through loud and clear.

Kelly O'Leary, endless source of personal information and everything on Andy, from training schedules to CDs and video clips, to show records and everything else I could possibly need to write the story of such an incredible animal, I thank you with all my heart.

I would also like to say an overdue thank you to Kathy Lowinger for saying "yes" to these books in the first place, and to Kathryn Cole for your constant, positive encouragement and help in making them happen. Pamela Osti, the most upbeat publicist in the world, thank you also. And to all the staff at Tundra who are involved in the making of these books – thank you so much. You are appreciated more than you know.

Contents

I

Wild Horse

Early dawn light shone softly on the mare's dark hide as she picked her way through the thick brush. Her shoulders and flanks were damp with sweat, and she paused now and then to listen, wait, and nip gently at her bulging sides. She had left the herd farther down in the valley and wandered up the mountainside alone, searching for just the right spot.

At last, she found it – a small clearing in the scrub where she would be hidden when she went down, where her foal would have time to gain strength before having to face the dangers of mustang life.

She wouldn't have to wait long. Thick, yellow milk dripped onto her hind legs as she grazed. The pains soon came more steadily. She was restless – lying down, standing up, pawing, and lying down again on her other side. When she went down the final time, the contractions were strong. With barely a sound, she pushed hard, pushed again, rested, and pushed once more. Her foal slipped onto the clean grass, and the pair lay still, exhausted. Life had begun for another wild horse in the Winnemucca area of Nevada.

The foal was a big one – a throwback to the heavy draft horses that had been turned loose amongst the wild Spanish mustangs when gas-powered machinery had become accessible to local farmers. The herd was a mix of many breeds, but continued to be known as mustangs, and they were as free and wild as their ancestors had been for almost two hundred years.

The colt was on his feet within half an hour of his birth, wobbling unsteadily to his mother's flank, searching for his first meal of rich, strength-giving milk. In a few hours, he had gained enough control of his long, spindly legs to trot sturdily beside his dam, even attempting a little leap or buck now and then. He tired quickly and needed to rest often, but before the day was over, the mare had led him back to the safety of the herd. A horse on its own was vulnerable.

The Winnemucca band was a healthy one. The Eugene Mountains, where they spent most of their time, were rugged and dry. Vegetation was sparse, but there were few predators, and the animals were hardy and well adapted. Their numbers were climbing steadily each year, sometimes forcing them to travel over large ranges in search of enough food and water. The colt was strong and ready to face the tough life that lay ahead.

He passed his first summer and autumn – wandering the desert-like valley and the mountainsides next to his mother, running and play-fighting with the other foals born that spring, and joining in the incessant hunt for nourishment. He watched as young stallions in their prime challenged the old. He learned the movements of combat as he played with the other foals. He learned the scent of the mountain lion and fled with the herd as the sounds of a newborn foal's agonizing squeals assaulted his ears and the smell of blood filled his nostrils. The herd taught him almost everything he'd need to know to survive in the wild. But they could not prepare him for what lay ahead. They could not teach him about humans.

The colt knew something of people. Their fences blocked the herd's progress at times, their cattle competed with the horses for grazing land, and men sometimes chased the herd away. The scent of humans was strong and distinctive, and, as they did with the mountain lion, the band stayed clear of them whenever possible.

But on a clear, crisp day in November 1985, they were not to be avoided. The Bureau of Land Management helicopter came early in the morning, loud and terrifying. The horses bolted and scattered, trying to seek refuge in the scrub and trees of the foothills where they were grazing. The helicopter moved quickly, blocking their way to cover. More than forty animals turned as one, and the band galloped down the pass toward the valley. The helicopter hovered behind them, low and menacing.

The colt tried to stay close to his mother as the herd pushed and crowded around him. The panicked flight of the horses slowed to a trot as they made their way across the rocky terrain. The helicopter hung back and didn't push, so long as the horses continued moving forward.

They trotted and loped until they were lathered and blowing, but the menacing machine did not go away.

Guided by subtle shifts of the helicopter, the horses were run into a shallow ravine. In the brush and trees surrounding them, tall, burlap fencing was visible and alarming, and the horses hesitated. A few animals scattered at the entrance as the scent of humans and their strange animals – horses, but not horses – wafted to them on the breeze, warning of danger. Before the rest of the herd could follow, the helicopter flew closer and dipped its tail, raising a dust cloud behind it. Tired, but freshly worried, the band broke into a gallop once more and charged into the ravine.

Everything happened quickly then. As the horses crowded farther into the enclosure, the fencing narrowed until there was nowhere left to go. The opening behind them was pulled closed and they were trapped. People on horseback and on foot were amongst them now, shouting, waving arms and whips, separating, and forcing them toward a narrow chute.

A man on his horse cut between the colt and his mother, pushing the colt toward the chute. In a blind panic, the colt tried to get back to the mare, but the man turned his horse into his path, cutting him off again and again, pushing him farther away. The colt had no choice but to follow the other young horses who moved up the ramp into a waiting trailer.

The youngsters, frightened and confused, jostled each other in the semi-darkness, seeking escape as the engine roared to life and the trailer rocked. Younger foals whinnied plaintively for their mothers, but the colt was quiet, bracing his legs and trembling with fear as the trailer bounced and swayed toward a sorting area fifteen minutes away.

At the sorting area, the horses were unloaded and driven, single file, through a series of chutes. The youngest foals were guided into a nursery pen where their mothers would soon join them. The foals old enough to be weaned, including the colt and the yearlings, were prodded toward another pen. Other youngsters were already there, having been brought from different trap sites. Throughout the morning more would arrive, until a few hundred horses milled in the pens, tired, confused, and anxious.

The colt listened intently over the chorus of whinnies for his mother's voice. Some of the youngsters paced frantically. One filly threw herself repeatedly at the fence, attempting to climb the barrier to reach her dam. Others, like the colt, stood quietly, listening. By night, the horses had settled. Only the occasional whinny echoed through the dark. The colt continued to listen, but his mother's voice didn't come to him. He would never hear her or see her again.

The next morning, the horses were loaded into another semi and shipped about a half hour south of Winnemucca to The National Wild Horse and Burro Center at Palomino Valley (PVC). There, they were run through chutes again and into a squeeze, where they had their hooves trimmed, were freeze branded on their necks, fitted with a leather collar and identification tags, vaccinated, and sorted according to age and sex. It all happened quickly, but by the time the colt was turned into his enclosure with the other weanling colts, he was shaken and exhausted. None of the defenses he had learned in the first six months of his life were helping him here. He couldn't run or fight or hide. So far, life with people was not much fun.

Human contact was minimal after that. Feed was delivered to the large pastures by truck, and the men observed the colts through binoculars. Any horse needing attention would be rounded up, driven to the chutes, and treated there. The colt was only brought in once, to be gelded. He came to know that time in the chutes meant separation from the security of the herd, some form of pain, and a great deal of fear. His strongest desire was to avoid those tight alleys and the people who were waiting there, as much as possible.

Without their families, the ability to travel, or the need to search for food, life had changed dramatically for the young horses. But they adapted, soon becoming accustomed to the new routine, following the feed truck eagerly, and spending their time in leisure play and rest. They would spend a much easier winter there, than they would have on the range. At PVC they could grow safely and change from shaggy babies into sleek, lanky yearlings.

The colt was watched carefully that winter and was often the subject of conversation amongst the people who worked at PVC. He stood out – tall, black, and impressive. He was leggy and somewhat awkward, but he moved with a long, flowing stride and had a soft, gentle expression. It was decided that he would be a good candidate for the Wild Horse Inmate Program (WHIP) at the Colorado State Prison in Canon City, CO. But he was too young to be trained. Instead, arrangements were made to ship him to a Bureau of Land Management (BLM) holding facility in Muleshoe, Texas, where he could mature.

The Muleshoe site was a state-of-the-art facility and the colt enjoyed a year of easy food, playful companionship with horses his own age, and relatively little disturbance by humans. He had grown accustomed to the sight and smell of men by now, and was less fearful of them. He was even becoming curious about them, sometimes sniffing a hand held out of a truck window or through a fence. He soon discovered those hands could feel good, scratching his face and around his ears, and that they sometimes held treats. But that was as far as it went. He was still wild, and except for the food they brought to his pasture, he had no fondness for people.

The colt grew tremendously that year, and by the spring of 1987, he was a full sixteen hands, much larger than most of the other two year olds. He was scruffy, skinny, and gawky, with huge feet and a big, drafty head. It was hard to tell what he might be good for, but the time had come to find out. In July, the big, black colt found himself in yet another semi with a group of other young horses, heading for prison.

2

Jail Bird Andy

crowd of men waited impatiently for the horses to arrive and be unloaded. They leaned on the metal fences of the small corrals, smoking, pointing at this horse and that, and calling out to each other roughly and jovially. The men were inmates who had been carefully selected and trained to participate in WHIP, a program organized by the BLM and prison officials to increase the adoptability of wild mustangs and provide a career training opportunity for the prisoners.

A man named Tommy was a part of the crowd that day. Stocky, tattooed, and mustached, Tommy was serving a life sentence for murder and was a fairly recent addition to the program. He had taken the training, had broke his first horse, and was now looking for his second.

Tommy, along with the other men, noticed the big colt right away. He couldn't be missed, standing a head taller than most of the others, his black coat gleaming with sweat. No one argued when Tommy claimed him. No one else wanted to take on such a big, wild horse.

Training started the next day. The colt was run into a tight chute, where he was fitted with a sturdy halter and handled all over. At first he fought hard, throwing himself against the bars of the chute, trying to rear, to bite, to kick – anything to rid himself of the hands that were touching him. He had learned early to hate the chutes, and he tried his hardest to escape. But the space was too small. He couldn't fight or get away. After a while, he stood still and allowed the handling. Only his trembling, blowing, and rolling eyes revealed his anger and fear.

When he had settled well enough in the chute, he was turned loose into the training corral, a long, thick rope attached to his halter with four men hanging on tight to the other end.

The men hung on while the colt pulled and twisted and fought to get away. The halter bit into his head, burning the thin skin behind his ears and across his nose, but still he fought, until the pain became too great. He stopped for a moment to rest, and the men moved closer, keeping the rope taut between them, the tension on his head steady. The man closest to him held out a hand and spoke gently to him. The colt pulled away again, but did not fight as strongly. A few more minutes, and he stopped again, and stretched his muzzle toward the hand. Instantly, the tension and the pain eased. As the man inched closer, the colt pulled back, and the pain of the halter returned.

Slowly, the man drew nearer until his fingertips brushed against the colt's muzzle. The colt jerked his head back, but didn't fight. He remembered the hands at the ranch – the gentle scratches and the treats. He reached out and sniffed cautiously at this man's fingers, explored them with his lips, then stood still as the hand rubbed his muzzle, moved farther up his face, scratching and rubbing the pain of the halter away. Before they were done, Tommy stood at the colt's shoulder, and the first stage of acceptance showed in the big horse's soft eyes.

It took a few weeks before Andy, as he was soon named, completely accepted the lessons Tommy taught him each day. The halter, the sacking out, having his feet picked up and worked with, having every part of his body handled, the saddle, the bridle, and finally a rider. Every step brought new terrors and took time and patience on Tommy's part. Andy experienced ropes, blindfolds, and a rider who would not come off, no matter how hard the colt bucked and twisted. But he also discovered a leader in Tommy, not so very different than the lead horse in a wild herd.

It was always easiest, and most comfortable, in the wild, to follow the leader's cues and the band rules. Andy, despite his size, had never been high in the pecking order of the herds he'd lived with, in the wild or at the BLM ranches. He was used to following. Once his initial panic subsided, he worked hard to reestablish that comfort level with this new "herd leader" and was soon working willingly with the men he had feared.

Ginger Scott, a part Cherokee horsewoman from Golden, Colorado, went to the prison just over a month after Andy had arrived, seeking a horse for herself and her daughter, Heather. Ginger and Heather lived in a house in the mountains where they were raising two wolves. Ginger was proud of her Native heritage and interested in living a life that honored it and helped to preserve a bit of American history. For her, a mustang was the natural choice of horse, although she knew there were easier and safer ways to acquire a horse. Little did she know that the horse she chose that day would far surpass her expectations and dreams.

Tony Bainbridge, the program's horse training supervisor that year, met Ginger when she arrived at the prison. Tony instructed Ginger not to engage in conversations with the prisoners, to fall to the ground immediately if he told her to, and to lock all of her personal belongings in her car. Feeling somewhat nervous, Ginger did as she was told (only to discover later that she had locked her keys in the car as well), and followed Tony to where the horses were waiting.

Ginger looked at many animals that day, but did not find any that were especially interesting to her. She was preparing to leave, when she spotted a big, gangly, black colt being ridden in a nearby field. She knew right away that she had found her horse. Both Tony and Tommy tried to talk her out of buying Andy, pointing out his oversized feet and enormous head. He was much too big and strong to be a woman's horse. She should keep looking.

But Ginger had made up her mind. His long, rocking-horse stride, willing disposition, and the gentle expression in his eyes clinched it for her. She paid one hundred and twenty-five dollars plus a pair of cowboy boots for Tommy, and became the first owner of the lanky, green-broke mustang. Andy's days of freedom were officially ended.

3

Dressage Horse

*T*able Mountain Ranch, in Golden, would be Andy's new home. Ginger and Heather were taking lessons there from a western trainer named Mark Boyle. They couldn't wait to start working with their new horse.

Table Mountain Ranch was a busy boarding and training facility, catering to several riding disciplines and providing specialized trainers for each. There was constant activity with horses and riders coming and going from the big indoor arena to the stables, working in the three outdoor paddocks or on the galloping track, preparing for trail rides, or for the shows that were held at the ranch on a regular basis. Idle horses relaxed in spacious, airy stalls, or grazed in the many paddocks and pastures on the property. Serious show riders owned many of these sleek, well-bred creatures. Wild mustangs were not the common fare, and Andy's arrival caused quite a stir.

Andy traveled in his first two-horse trailer for this trip – a step up from the dark, crowded semis he had experienced up to now. Ginger fitted him with a head-guard in case he became upset and hit his head on the trailer. He accepted it patiently, but it proved to be unnecessary. He still didn't like traveling, but he had lost his terror of trailers, and the short trip from Canon City to Golden was uneventful.

The barn manager, Connie, was anxious about this newcomer. How would a mustang fit in with the other horses? What would he be like to handle and deal with on a daily basis? Her worries were not eased when the enormous, rather homely colt was led off the trailer, head high, prancing, and snorting in alarm at the crowd that had gathered to see him. Connie slowly exhaled the breath she had been holding and resignedly directed Ginger to a pen near the stable. They would keep Andy isolated until they had a better idea what he was like.

It didn't take long to find out. Within a week, everyone at the stable who dealt with Andy realized that he was not dangerous. He was easily frightened – everything was so new to him. He was lonely. He had never been on his own before and he was vulnerable and nervous. He was like an outcast young stallion, banned from the herd. He began to turn to the humans in his life, seeking the security of a new "herd." He was innately gentle and eager to please, and he quickly gained everyone's trust and affection.

Andy was soon turned into a larger pasture with several other horses, including a twelve-year-old Morgan gelding called Hawk. Hawk was often brought to the pasture by a tiny woman with a freckled face, quick smile, and pleasant voice. She noticed that Andy was often on his own – the bottom of the pecking order – and she sometimes made a point of giving him a bit of attention. In time, the little woman and the big, black horse would become an inseparable team, although neither of them knew it then.

After working with Andy and Ginger just a couple of times, it became clear to Mark Boyle that Andy was not a typical mustang and was not suited for western riding. He was simply too big and rangy for the tight, fast movements required of a western mount. Mark advised

Ginger to concentrate on getting some weight on the colt and suggested she try him as a dressage horse.

"He's so darned skinny," laughed Mark. "It's like his body hasn't caught up with his head and feet yet. But he's got that nice, big stride. He might just do okay in dressage."

Ginger, who was a western rider, took on the challenge of learning dressage gamely, and spent the rest of that autumn and winter working with a trainer named Diana Smith, learning the basics and having fun with her newest family member.

Andy got used to the confinement of stalls, the tickle of kisses on his muzzle, the high-pitched voices and gentle hands of the women who cared for him, and the hustle and bustle of the stable. He put on some weight. His coat shone richly from the good diet and regular grooming he received. And he kept on growing, adding another three inches to his already tall frame. He was growing more handsome and tamer with every passing day.

By spring, Diana was seeing something in Andy that indicated he might be more than just an average horse. Ginger didn't have the skills to advance his work at that time, so Diana suggested they look for someone who could – just to test him out.

Diana was working with another woman that winter, a serious dressage rider named Kelly O'Leary. Kelly was young, just twenty-one years old, recently married, and a very dedicated horsewoman. Kelly's horse, Cambridge Winterhawk, Hawk for short, had come up lame, and Kelly was looking for a horse to work with. Diana introduced the two women and Ginger agreed to let Kelly work with Andy to see what she thought of him. Kelly started riding him in May.

Andy and Kelly were a bit of an odd couple at first. Kelly was petite and looked even tinier astride the enormous three year old. He was awkward, unbalanced, and lacked strength in the hind end. She didn't have the legs to wrap around his wide girth to cue him easily. He was still too thin for his size and his head was half the size of his rider. There was still much to learn about him.

But Kelly quickly discovered an intelligent, cooperative, willing soul in Andy, and he responded to the same qualities in her. They had much to overcome if they were to go the distance in dressage, but the initial connection between the pair was strong and promising. Kelly agreed to work with him that year and see what they could accomplish.

Competitive dressage involves the careful advancement in training of a horse over a number of years, with several levels of progression, each more demanding and difficult than the last. At its highest levels, the performance of the horse can be stunningly beautiful and has been compared to ballet. Only the most skilled riders and horses with very good conformation and muscle control reach these higher levels. Never before had a mustang made it to upper-level dressage competition. Many people were doubtful that it would happen now, and even Kelly and Ginger weren't sure it was possible. Still, they were curious to see just how far the big colt could progress.

Kelly and Andy worked hard that first year together, mastering the basic forward movements required at Training Level and early First Level. Always, Ginger was there, grooming Andy, admiring her big boy as Kelly put him through his paces, riding him herself, and loving him. Kelly and Ginger became good friends and shared their dreams about Andy and what they hoped he could do. It was still a big "wait and see," but they were ready to take the first step. Table Mountain Ranch was hosting a United States Dressage Federation (USDF) competition that summer and they decided to enter Andy, just to see what would happen.

By the day of the show, Andy was ready. Consistent riding over the past year had developed his muscles, although he still had some filling out to do. Excellent care had brought out the sheen of his pitch-black coat, and exposure to the activity around the stable had settled his nervousness. He looked the part of a dressage horse, and few could guess his breed or heritage, although Kelly and Ginger were always proud to let curious people know he was a mustang. They delighted in the shocked looks that always came over people's faces.

Andy had come a long way in a year, but part of him remained on the Nevada range. He submitted to the work of people, always willing, always trying his best. He enjoyed the easy meals and gentle grooming he received daily. But he had not fully connected with humans, nor was he affectionate in the way of domestic-born horses. He remained aloof and quiet, showing only glimmers of the personality inside.

He was beginning to communicate with the people closest to him. If he was confused about Kelly's cues while she rode him, he would shake his great head back and forth until she was clearer, or broke the exercise down into simpler steps. Sometimes, while being groomed, he would rest his head against Kelly or Ginger, and hold it there while they wrapped their arms around him in a horsy hug. But most of the time he stood quietly, submitting, absorbing, and giving little of himself away.

On show day, Andy was patient as Kelly and Ginger worked, bathing him, polishing his hooves, and braiding his thick mane. When they were finished, Andy was immaculate and handsome – every inch a show horse, ready for his first test. The thin, scruffy young mustang with the tangled mane and the unkempt hooves was nowhere to be seen. The only thing he lacked was a fancy name like all the other horses in the show ring.

Ginger decided that Andy needed a more refined name that befitted a show horse, yet she didn't want something too stuffy. She chose JB Andrew – JB stood for jailbird! Now, he was ready.

In dressage, horses are tested individually on transitions, obedience, suppleness, gait quality (balance and energy), and the rider's use of aids, which should be nearly imperceptible. A good dressage horse will respond to the lightest aids: a squeeze of the leg, a touch of the spur, a closing of the fingers, or a subtle shift in the rider's weight. Every movement and transition is scored from zero to ten by the judges, then tallied at the end of the performance. Each level has a number of tests that must be passed before the horse can move to the next level. Andy was being judged on the first test in First Level.

He did better than expected for a newcomer. Calm as a seasoned horse, JB Andrew worked through the steps of the test beautifully, and at the end of the show, he finished fourth out of the twenty competitors.

Ginger and Kelly were thrilled and decided that it was time to take Andy's dressage career seriously. How far he could progress was yet to be seen and the ladies were eager to find out. He was certainly showing promise.

4

Champion

ndy would compete at First Level during the 1990 show season, and he'd make it perfectly clear that he had found his niche. Early in the year, Kelly began attending clinics run by Jan Ebeling, a well-respected German dressage trainer working out of Capricorn Stable, just a short distance from Table Mountain Ranch. Jan was a rising star in the dressage world and Kelly was excited to have him work with Andy.

Jan was impressed with the big horse and under his guidance, the team prepared to take on the dressage elite.

Once or twice a week, Kelly would ride Andy to Capricorn Stables with Ginger following behind in her car in case they ran into problems. The roadwork was good for Andy, a nice break from the routine of the arena, but a near wreck gave the girls a change of heart.

Andy was traveling at a comfortable trot, relaxed and settled, as he had come to know the route to Capricorn Stables well. Kelly rode with a loose rein and was enjoying the ride. Ginger followed slowly. Suddenly, the sound of a siren startled them all out of their peacefulness, and before another few moments had passed, a fire truck was bearing down on them. At the same time, a dog came running out of its driveway, barking at the noise of the truck, and Andy spooked into the road.

Luckily, the fire truck had passed them mere seconds before Andy was on the road, but it was too close a call for Kelly and Ginger. Soon after, Andy was moved to Capricorn Stables.

Andy wouldn't stay at Capricorn for long, though. Capricorn Stables had a new owner around that time, and this person quickly displeased Kelly and Ginger by having a vet give Andy his required vaccinations without their permission. Kelly had already scheduled her vet to come out and do the job, and a bit of a tiff followed. The feelings between owner and client were never fully repaired and, within a few months, Andy was on the move again.

The big horse spent a short time at Blue Mountain Ranch, also in Golden, and then moved to Andover Farm, a Morgan breeding establishment run by Cindy Vogels, a friend of Kelly's.

The lives of the women in Andy's life were hectic. Kelly's husband had left his job to complete his schooling, and the couple were living off the income Kelly earned working for her parents in their mail-order business. She was also attending school part-time, and training horses. Ginger had recently divorced her husband and was working two jobs to support herself and her daughter and to pay for Andy's expenses. Finances played a big part in the frequent moves and choices of stables, but Andy's welfare was always their first priority and his care never suffered wherever they went.

Andy took all the changes in stride, continuing to train well and compete even better. Kelly was so confident in his abilities that she took out lifetime memberships with the three major dressage associations: the local Rocky Mountain Dressage Society (RMDS), the United States Dressage Federation (USDF), and the American Horse Show Association (AHSA). People were beginning to pay attention to the unusual horse who entered the show ring so majestically, not just because of his striking looks and strange background, but also because of his talent in dressage.

By the end of 1990, after being judged on all four tests at First Level, in only eight shows, Andy had accumulated enough points to rank thirty-seventh out of almost sixteen hundred horses competing through the USDF. He won the Region 8 AHSA Championship, First Level.

This was impressive, but many people were quick to point out that it was also the easiest level. Lots of horses that do well at the start of their careers and look like stars fade as the levels get tougher. Only time would tell if JB Andrew had what it took to get to the top.

When Andy was not training or competing, Kelly and Ginger tried to provide as much natural "horse time" as possible, always respecting his wild heritage. He was never as relaxed in the confinement of stalls, although he had grown well-accustomed to them. Everywhere he went, the ladies insisted on having him live at pasture – a very unusual situation for a serious, competitive dressage horse.

His calm and gentle nature proved useful at Andover Farm, where he soon earned the job of weanling babysitter. Weanlings are often left in the care of a quiet gelding when then are taken from their mothers, to help calm them, teach them adult horse rules, and provide them with safe companionship. Andy loved the job.

Cindy Vogels was nervous at first about putting Andy in with the fine-boned Morgan babies. One kick from the massive black horse could be fatal. But Andy never kicked. He tolerated the youngsters' playfulness like a kind old uncle, allowing them to strike their tiny hooves against his sturdy ribs, nibble his ears, and nip at his muscular neck and legs. If they became too unruly, he would simply pin his ears and shake his mighty head at them, and they would scatter. He was a mature five year old now, and for the first time in his life, he was at the top of the pecking order.

And he would stay that way, in more ways than one.

Kelly continued to be under pressure as her young husband worked through school and they struggled to get by on her limited income. Kelly was still working Andy and Hawk with Jan Ebeling, but Jan and his partner would soon be moving to California. Jan's girlfriend had been working with the horses of an arteriovascular surgeon and horseman named Dennis Law. Dennis was one of the first owners of a warmblood dressage horse in the Colorado area and was deeply involved in the dressage world. Now there was a job opening at his stable, and Kelly decided to apply.

Dennis had a reputation for keeping his grooms for no more than two years. Kelly wanted a chance to work for him, seeing it as a perfect opportunity to advance her own career in horses. Grooms in Dennis's stable received a bonus of free lessons with professional dressage trainer/rider Sue Halasz, and Kelly wanted this badly. Besides, she really needed the extra money.

Dennis's stable was located in Littleton, just south of Golden, in a very wealthy neighborhood. Kelly settled into an apartment attached to the barn, moved Hawk into Dennis's stable and, soon, Andy followed. At Dennis's, both Kelly and Andy found stability and friendship. Despite Dennis's promise of a two-year job, this was the place they would call home for the next seven years.

Andy was training now for Second Level competition, requiring the forward and basic sideways movements of First Level, but adding a medium and extended trot, as well as more collection, or hind-end compulsion, and self-carriage. Andy had finally filled out his almost seventeen-hand frame, topping off at over eighteen hundred pounds, and his head and feet were more in proportion to his body. The BLM brand on his powerful, arched neck was the only remaining clue to his wonderful background. He was every inch a strong, beautiful, dressage horse.

Kelly began clinicing with Claus Neilson, a Swedish dressage trainer, and working on Andy's overall strength. There was a notable drop in competitors by Third Level, and Kelly knew that if Andy were to make it past this point, he would need to be as physically strong as possible.

From Dennis's, Kelly could access the High Line Canal trail system, and much of Andy's conditioning took place there, trotting along the trails and working in the water, against the flow. This, combined with three or four days a week of arena work, and extra training time with Claus or Sue, prepared Andy, mentally and physically, for the competitions ahead.

Ginger remained heavily involved in Andy's care, attending every show she could and helping Kelly with preparations. She still rode him, and even tried her hand at showing him in a couple of First Level tests. Mostly, she loved him with all her heart. Watching him perform brought tears to her eyes almost every time. She could hardly believe that this majestic black horse, moving so elegantly around the show ring, was the hundred-and-twenty-five-dollar mustang she'd picked out of the scruffy prison herd. She was extremely proud of him.

She had every reason to be. By the time all points had been accumulated, shows won, and the season ended, Andy had placed twentieth nationally with USDF out of eleven hundred and sixty-two competitors. He earned the AHSA Zone 8 Championship, the USDF Region 5 Reserve Championship, and placed third with the RMDS. JB Andrew was at the top of his game.

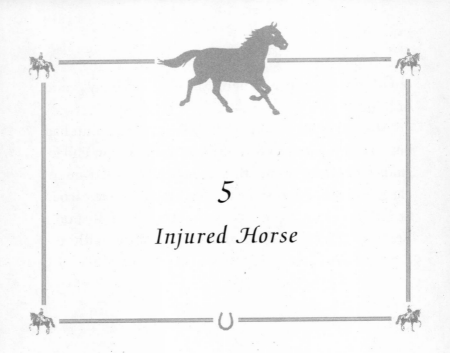

5

Injured Horse

Kelly and Ginger looked forward to the 1992 show season eagerly, but with some trepidation. This was the tough year, the one that tended to separate the very good horses from the so-so horses. Kelly had not made it past Third Level with Hawk, but she was feeling confident that Andy could rise to the challenge.

Andy was beginning to change. The change was so gradual that no one really noticed at first, but it was there. Andy was learning to love people, just as they loved him. He was beginning to pay attention to the activity around him – not yet fully interacting, but watching with interest. Occasionally, he would seek attention, purposefully nudging Kelly or Ginger, pushing his head toward them for a hug, nuzzling Kelly's neck or hair, or searching for the treats he had come to expect.

Andy was excellent at reading Kelly's moods. He normally greeted her eagerly at his pasture gate with a hearty whinny, but if she arrived in a grumpy mood, he would walk to the other side of the field and refuse to see her. Kelly soon learned that the time she spent with Andy was for Andy alone. All of her stresses, worries, and negative feelings had to be left behind. He was good for her that way.

Andy also became protective of Kelly and jealous if she gave attention to the other animals in the pasture. He would chase them away, biting them on the chest if they persisted in visiting with her. Andy had claimed Kelly as his and, gradually, the pair were changing from horse and rider to partners. This would be most important in the years ahead as an excellent dressage performance comes from the rider and horse being as one, each trusting the other, and connecting on a mental/emotional level. Kelly and Andy were connecting.

The focus in Third Level competition is on *collection*. A horse normally carries a greater amount of weight on its front legs, but shifts its weight to the hind to spin, rear, or move in an animated way, as a stallion will do to show off for a mare. This shift in weight and power to the hind end is called collection. It causes the horse to move in a compacted, controlled, but highly energized way. It is demanding on the muscles and joints and a horse needs to be physically mature and fit to withstand the rigors of this training. Andy also needed to add the extended trot and canter, a single flying change, and a half pirouette – all challenging movements. Andy was ready.

Claus Neilson continued to come to Dennis's stable to work with Kelly and Andy. He taught Kelly the crucial skill of handling her dressage whip. A perfectly timed and placed touch of the whip (used only lightly, to cue the horse in ways that her hands and short legs could not) made all the difference in Andy's response. The whip was not carried in competition, but was useful as a training tool in the arena, combined with the hand, leg, and weight cues, making the cues crystal clear and the responses immediate and smooth.

When JB Andrew entered the show ring that season, he looked as though he was ready to continue his impressive winning streak of the past two years. He did well in the first tests at Third Level and looked stronger with every performance. But he only competed in five shows early that year, before a serious injury threatened to end his promising career.

Andy's best friend at this point in his life was a shaggy brown mule called Mr. Mule. Mr. Mule had been Andy's pasture mate for the past year, and they had bonded quickly and deeply. Andy was always excited to get back to his pasture and Mr. Mule after being away for training or a show.

One day, Kelly was turning Andy out, and in his eagerness to get to Mr. Mule he spun and spooked himself, cracking his right hind fetlock hard against the heavy wooden frame of the gate. In that split second, it looked like Andy's career, if not his life, might be over.

He was so lame, refusing to bear any weight at all on the leg, that Kelly was certain he must have broken it. A broken leg is serious for a horse – almost always fatal. Kelly was devastated as she slowly led Andy back to the stable, one painful, hopping step at a time. She thought nothing about the competitions coming up, or the fact that Andy's career might be over. She thought only of his pain and how empty her life would be without him in it. She hoped they would be able to do something to help him.

Kelly phoned Ginger and the veterinarian. For the next few hours they worked together, soothing, X-raying,

icing, and wrapping the leg – and praying that the big horse would be all right.

The X-rays brought good news; no break! The vet diagnosed a severe bone bruise and recommended cold wraps and pain medication for a few days, followed by stall rest and hand walking over the next few weeks. "These things tend to heal slowly," the vet told them. "I doubt if he'll be back in competition this season."

That didn't matter to Kelly and Ginger. They were simply relieved to know that the horse that had become so much a part of their lives was going to be all right.

* * *

Andy recovered slowly, and went back into light training more than a month later. Collection work was avoided at first to prevent straining the hind leg joints. It would take several more weeks before he was ready to return to his normal training routine. They had to go slowly. Andy had lost some of his conditioning because of the stall time and he needed to be built back up before he could safely manage the required movements. Would he be able to come back? Would the injured joint plague his career? Only time would answer that question.

Kelly and Claus worked with Andy that winter, and Andy responded to the renewed training gamely, mastering the Third Level movements and training for Fourth

Level. At Fourth Level he was introduced to the double bridle and he needed to be able to do three sequence changes, or changing the leading leg at the canter every three or four strides. Andy found this movement easy and seemed to enjoy it. He was ready to try again.

Andy competed at Third and Fourth Level in 1993, completing the Third Level tests he had missed the year before and beginning the Fourth Level series. He looked good, competing strongly, with no sign of the injury holding him back. It was a sight to see – the great black horse, carrying his diminutive rider, entering the dressage ring with long, powerful strides, neck arched proudly, and extraordinary self-control.

Kelly rode the tests carefully. The pair endured the seven minutes of intense concentration like the professionals they were, taking care not to miss any required movements:

Enter at A collected trot to X. Halt. Salute. Proceed collected trot to C. Track right to M. Medium trot to K. Collected trot to F. Half pass left, F-X. At X, circle left 8m, then straight ahead. At I, halt, rein back four steps, proceed immediately, collected canter, left lead, to C. Track left to H. Medium canter to K. Collected canter to F. Half pass left, F-X. From I, circle left 10m, then straight ahead to C. Track left to H. Collected walk to S. Extended walk to P. Collected walk to F. Turn right. Between D & K, half pirouette right, proceed collected walk. Between D & F, half pirouette left, proceed collected walk. Turn left. Collected walk to A. Collected canter, left lead. A-C, Serpentine in four loops, width of arena, the first and last loops true canter, the second and third counter canter with simple lead change at X. At M, extended canter to F. Collected canter to K. Half pass right, K-X. At I, circle right 10m, then straight ahead. At G, collected trot to C. Track left to H. Extended trot to F. Collected trot to K. Half pass right, K-X. At X, circle right 8m. Straight ahead to G. Halt. Salute. Exit, free walk, long rein at A.

It was hard work, but they did well.

The number of horses competing nationally at this level had, predictably, dropped drastically. By season's end, Andy had placed a respectable eighty-fourth out of seven hundred and fifty-seven with USDF at Third Level. This was an impressive accomplishment, considering only a portion of his classes entered that year were at Third Level, limiting his ability to rack up points. Kelly and Ginger were very pleased and decided to push on.

Kelly celebrated for another reason that fall. After ten years of classes fit in between work, horses, and marriage, she graduated from college with a finance degree. It felt good to have school behind her. She faced that winter with high spirits, strong hopes, and plans for the future.

*　*　*

Andy didn't receive the championship ribbon that year, but he had caught the attention of the media. For most of the people who knew him, Andy's heritage had become secondary to his talent in the dressage arena. But for the spectators who came to watch the shows, and for Ginger and Kelly, the fact that he was a mustang remained a source of interest and pride. People were amazed that a mustang could look like Andy and perform like JB Andrew.

The people at the Bureau of Land Management (BLM) were keeping track, too. Constantly seeking ways to increase public interest in mustang adoptions, they began to promote Andy's achievements. Andy appeared on Channel 4 News in a feature about the BLM and the ways they work to control the mustang population. It would be the first of many public appearances, and it was the beginning of a shift in his career from dressage star to mustang ambassador.

6

Kelly's Horse

ndy continued to train at Fourth Level in 1994. He also began preparing for Prix St. George (PSG), improving his sequence changes and doing a longer series of them. He mastered the difficult canter pirouette and would compete at both levels that year.

The step up to Prix St. George was huge, "a really big deal" as Kelly put it, as this is the first International Equestrian Federation (FEI) level, and rather elite. No other mustang had ever gone this far in competition. The animals at this level are almost all carefully bred

European horses – warmbloods and thoroughbreds with impeccable pedigrees – dressage bred into their very genes. Kelly could hardly believe that Andy had made it this far. She was nearly sick at times from nerves, but Andy settled her fears, doing his best, as always, and doing well. He finished the season in the top third of the six hundred and sixty-two horses that competed nationally at the PSG Level.

Although Andy was continuing to rise in the dressage ranks (and this would remain an important part of his life in the coming years), 1994 marked a definite transition in his career. The media attention he had received the previous season had sparked public interest in him – as a talented dressage horse, and even more, as a mustang. A greater than usual number of spectators began to attend the shows to see the massive black "wild" horse and talented dressage competitor. The BLM was pleased, setting up a booth at show sites to cope with the growing flood of questions about JB Andrew and how interested people could adopt a mustang.

The BLM put out a trading card for Andy and released a small book through the Denver Museum of Natural History Wonder Series. It was only the start, but Andy was becoming a celebrity.

While fortunes rose for Andy, the people who loved

him were facing challenges that would change their futures forever.

Kelly's father passed away in 1995, leaving a tremendous gap in her life. Her mother quickly decided to sell the mail-order business to a friend. Kelly continued to work there, but it was not the same without her dad, and she began to focus more heavily than ever on her career with horses.

Ginger was running into troubles of her own. She lost one of her jobs, which left her struggling to get by as a single mom. When she had a difficult time finding other work, she knew there were some tough decisions to make. Andy was an expensive horse to keep, despite the fact that Kelly never charged her for training him. Board, medical care, farrier, equipment, and show fees . . . they all added up to a lot of extra money. With great sadness, Ginger decided that she must sell her beautiful mustang.

Kelly was beside herself when Ginger told her the news. "You can't sell him, Ginger! He's your horse and my horse. He belongs with us. He's come so far with us."

Ginger had tears in her eyes as she listened to Kelly's pleas, but she really had no choice.

Kelly was sick with worry. She didn't want to lose the beautiful horse who had become so important in her life. She decided that she must buy him herself. Where on earth would she come up with the fifteen thousand dollars Ginger was asking for him? She and her husband were still struggling themselves, paying off school loans and living on a limited income. Her husband had graduated with an accounting degree, but had not yet found a job in his field. He worked, instead, for his father's travel agency business, developing accounting software for the industry. Kelly continued to work two jobs, but even with all of that, they were barely getting by, and there was no way they could come up with the money needed to buy Andy.

Ginger was elated when Kelly confided her wish to buy Andy. "That would be perfect. I've been so worried about sending him to people who don't know him. And this way, I could still see him and be in his life. I mean, he's practically yours anyway."

The girls talked more seriously about it then, and Ginger agreed to sell him to Kelly for only five thousand dollars, since Kelly had put in so much training and had made him worth so much in the first place.

Everything was looking up ... until Kelly's husband, Dave, flat out refused to put up five thousand dollars for the horse. It was still a lot of money, and it was money they didn't have. Nothing could persuade him, and it looked like Andy might have to be sold to someone else.

Kelly was depressed, and it showed. When her mother found out what was happening, she offered to help. She knew how much her daughter loved Andy, and she was as interested in the elegant black mustang as the rest of the local public. Secretly, Kelly's mother paid the five thousand dollars for Andy, and a story was created for Dave about how Ginger couldn't bear to let Andy go to strangers and so, had given him to Kelly. Dave was convinced, and Andy had a new owner – his own Kelly.

* * *

Ginger was heartbroken at having to give up her horse. Within a few short months, she had lost her job, her horse, and the day she signed Andy's papers over to Kelly, her last wolf died of cancer. Life couldn't get much lower. She wondered if things would ever balance out for her again. It didn't seem possible on that day.

In the following months, Ginger had difficulty even visiting Andy and Kelly. It was hard for her to see the beautiful horse that was once hers and know he belonged to someone else now, even a good friend like Kelly. It took time, but gradually her pain began to ease. She returned to his life again, as his biggest fan, and frequent helper at shows and the stable, but it was never quite the same for her. She was glad for Andy though, because as far as he knew, nothing had changed. For him, life was constant, with wonderful care, a steady climb to the top, and a solid, growing base of fans cheering him along.

7

Mustang Ambassador

Andy would reach full-fledged celebrity status in 1996. He would not compete this year, training, instead, for the very difficult Intermediare 1 Level, which required even greater collection, sequence changes at every two strides (later at every stride), and a full one-eighty-degree canter pirouette. The movements required enormous strength and control, and Andy needed the extra year of training before he would be ready to compete at this level.

He would not be out of the public eye, however. In fact, the people of Colorado would get to know JB Andrew very well in the next couple of years.

Andy and Kelly were invited to perform at The National Western Stock Show in January, to promote the mustang breed and demonstrate the *Kur* — a beautiful dressage freestyle, performed to music.

This was their first non-competitive show, their first promotional invitation, and at this show, Kelly was introduced to an Andy she had never met before. He was very extroverted, demanding attention from the crowds that flocked to his stall to see him. He seemed to understand that he was important, and he loved it. The aloof mustang of the past was long gone. Kelly had to watch carefully, as Andy was offered everything from cookies and doughnuts, to soda pop and beer. He swallowed it all, including one lady's acrylic fingernail!

In the show ring, he performed with such power and elegance that the crowd was spellbound. He was so animated in his extended trot that he seemed to float above the ground. He completed his sequence changes with ease and grace, his diagonal movements smoothly, and his collected canter with incredible control and power. His neck was arched proudly and his enormous hooves

kept perfect time with the music, "The Good, The Bad, and The Ugly."

At the end, the applause was loud and appreciative. Andy puffed up and trotted around the ring, animated and showing off. For the first time, he seemed to know that the clapping was for him, and he moved like Kelly had never felt him move before. Dave was in the stands that day and later reported that Andy looked amazing. The crowd loved him.

Later on, when things had quieted down, Kelly was wandering the fairgrounds and came across a booth called Briarpatch. It was covered with model horses – Breyer models – of all breeds and colors. Mares, foals, and stallions, working horses, and famous horses of the past. As Kelly stood and ran her fingers across the smooth coats of the plastic figurines, she was transported back in time to her childhood in Miami, Florida.

She had been horse crazy, like so many girls her age, and lived and breathed horses. She read every book she could find about the beautiful creatures, including veterinary manuals, but her parents felt it was unkind to own a horse in Miami. The heat and bugs were hard on horses there, they said.

A doctor, treating Kelly for eardrum problems, had given her a model horse, her first Breyer. It was a gray mare in a running position, with its full tail streaming out behind her. Kelly had been infatuated with it – with the perfectly shaped head, the delicate legs, the glossy coat, and smooth muscles. She carefully took it from home to home as she moved – from Miami to Maine, and, finally, to Colorado. It wasn't until then that she finally realized her dream of owning a horse of her own and bought Hawk. Nevertheless, the model horse still stood, chipped but treasured, on her bedroom shelf, a symbol of a special dream hard come by.

A smile spread across Kelly's face as an idea formed in her mind. When she looked up, her eyes had lost the faraway dreaminess and were focused and determined. She asked the person who was manning the booth who she would have to talk to if she wanted to have a Breyer model made of her horse.

As it turned out, Peter Stone, whose grandfather had started the Breyer company, was in the booth to sign models. Kelly approached him and told him Andy's story. Mr. Stone asked to see Andy and was very impressed with him. He agreed to make a model of the mustang. It would be one of the only models ever released of a horse who was still alive.

Kelly was elated. Somehow, this was the pinnacle for her. Of all the shows, the points earned, the ribbons –

nothing stood up to this. This was the culmination of all her lifelong dreams. In her mind, at that moment, Andy had made it!

The Breyer model (#943) of JB Andrew would be released that spring. Kelly arranged for a video to be made of Andy, including footage of the WHIP program and of Ginger and herself bringing him along in the dressage world. She would sell this, and the model, at promotional shows over the next two years.

JB Andrew performed at the Horse Expo and High Prairie Farms that year, thrilling crowds with his energetic musical freestyle. The interest he created in the mustang breed, and in wild horse adoptions, was tremendous. He appeared on three news channels, one telling the story of his old prison trainer, Tommy, and Andy's own rise to fame, and the others promoting the BLM mustangs and Andy's National Stock Show appearance. He was featured in several prominent horse magazines, including *Dressage Today*, *Western Horseman*, *Horse Play*, and *Chronicle of the Horse*. His story appeared in a collection of horse stories called *From Mustangs to Movie Stars*. His image appeared on T-shirts, sweatshirts, and ball caps. Andy was famous!

But life was not all fun and games for the horse or

Kelly. They were training hard for Intermediare 1 and 2 and the pace was vigorous.

Kelly's home life continued to be financially unstable, as Dave and his father worked to complete a second computer program for the travel industry. This time, Dave was not getting paid for his work. Money was very tight.

At the same time, it was getting harder to keep Andy, who was now twelve years old, sound. He had developed a type of arthritis known as ringbone, and he needed regular Legend shots to maintain the synovial fluids in his joints. The farrier who worked on Andy's feet began making subtle changes to the angle of his hooves, believing it would help, but Kelly was concerned. Even slight angle changes could add unnecessary stress to Andy's ligaments and leave him prone to injury. She discussed her concerns with the farrier, but he didn't see the problem and continued to shoe Andy wrong.

Kelly asked for help from her vet, who X-rayed Andy to prove to the farrier why his style of trimming and shoeing could be detrimental. The X-rays showed that the balance of the foot was, indeed, wrong. In the end, Kelly had resolved the problem, but, between this and the routine veterinary care he required now, Kelly had wracked up a bill of over eight thousand dollars. She and Dave were on the brink of financial disaster.

Luckily, Dave's father sold the computer program just in time, and Dave took a temporary job with a large company in Florida. The young couple was saved from going under once again, but the strain had taken a toll on them.

Andy and Kelly were working harder than they ever had before. The movements required of Andy at Intermediare 1 put great strain on his legs, back, and muscles. Kelly was devoted, willing to do whatever it took to keep him fit, happy, and injury-free. To her, he was worth every minute, every dollar, and every worried, sleepless night she spent. He had become her soul mate. He had proven to her that anything was possible if you worked hard enough for it. She would never give him up, and she would never give up on him.

Andy didn't let her down. In 1997, he competed at Intermediare 1 against some of the country's best dressage horses. He was doing the piaffe and passage (extremely collected trotting movements), full one-eighty-degree canter pirouettes, and single stride sequence changes. Andy was stunning to watch; a shining black powerhouse, contained and in perfect unison with his tiny rider. By season's end, he ranked one hundred and twenty-fifth out of nearly four hundred and fifty competitors. He was still doing very well.

The BLM continued to use Andy to promote mustang adoptions that year, and these were the shows Kelly and Andy enjoyed the most. Performing the Kur for the general public was far different from riding a test for the judges. The pressure was off, the music moved them, and the crowds were always extremely appreciative, perhaps not really fully understanding what they were watching, but always impressed by the wild mustang dancing his wonderful routine for them.

The pair was invited to the Rangely County Fair to protest against the illegal rounding up and killing of wild mustangs by farmers. The BLM also arranged a special appearance for them at the prestigious, annual Dressage at Devon Show in Pennsylvania, paying all their expenses and setting up an information booth to handle questions.

This would be a tougher crowd to please, as most of the spectators were there to watch the dressage competitions and were knowledgeable about what they were seeing. And fewer of them knew of JB Andrew. Kelly was nervous at first. It was their first time showing out of their own state, and she knew that some of the best riders in the East would be there.

Kelly stayed close to Andy, alone and quiet in his stall, going over the ride in her mind, as was her habit before each competition. Andy stood patiently as she brushed his coat to a polished shine, listening as she recited the sequence of movements.

Suddenly, as though to tell her to knock it off and relax, he pushed his head toward her, nearly knocking her off her feet. She caught her balance, laughing, and wrapped her arms around the beautiful big head. His forehead pushed hard against her chest. She felt better and was ready to face the Devon crowd.

Andy was a success, sparking a great deal of surprise and interest when it was announced that he was a mustang, who once roamed wild in the mountains of Nevada. The spectators were enthusiastic and, once again, the big horse's stable area was swamped with fans after the demonstration. Breyer models and videos were sold, trading cards and information pamphlets were handed out, and Andy enjoyed his fair share of treats and attention.

JB Andrew, gentle mustang ambassador, was the happiest and most loved wild horse America had ever known.

8

Top of the Pecking Order

ndy and Kelly did not compete in 1998. Andy was improving his Intermediare work and training at Grand Prix Level – the highest level of competitive dressage. Kelly, who had been suffering from carpal tunnel syndrome for several years (a common affliction in the horse industry), underwent surgery to repair the overworked tendons in her arm, putting her out of riding commission for a while.

Sue Halasz, who had been working occasionally with the pair since they had come to Dennis's stable, took over some of Andy's training for a while. When Andy was invited back to the National Western Stock Show to do a dressage demonstration that year, Sue agreed to ride in Kelly's place.

Sue was no stranger to the show ring, but she had never performed for a crowd like this before. Instead of the polite applause that followed a dressage test, there was thunderous, enthusiastic, long-lasting clapping, hoots, hollers, and whistles. Swarms of little girls followed Sue and Andy back to the stable, flooding Sue with questions, patting Andy's nose, and staring up at him with dreamy eyes.

Sue was completely out of her element and quite overwhelmed. But she soon found herself enjoying the crowds and the attention as much as Andy, and she had a very good time.

Andy participated in several other promotional events that year, including the Parade of Animals, sponsored by the Morris Animal Foundation (an organization devoted to raising funds for animal health-care research). There, they met Betty White, star of the TV sitcom *The Golden Girls*, and animal lover supreme. Once again, Andy appeared on Channel 4 News, this time towering over the petite Betty White while she spoke about the Morris Foundation fundraiser.

For Kelly, the year signaled a time for change, once again. She was feeling restless at Dennis's. She had not advanced in her training career as much as she had hoped, had suffered a few disappointments, and was feeling the tension of a dying relationship between Dennis and his wife. There were no big, solid reasons for moving this time. It was simply time to go.

In December, Kelly took a job at the luxurious Southern Pines Farm, in Parker, Colorado. Andy was soon right at home in the large pastures, spacious stalls, and enormous indoor arena. Kelly's own marriage was showing signs of strain around this time. The change and challenges of a new stable helped keep her spirits up and her mind focused on the future.

Kelly and Andy returned to competition in 1999, entering classes in Intermediare 1 and 2, and the Kur. Andy, as always, did his best, thrilling spectators with his powerful, fluid gaits and skillful handling of the difficult movements. By year's end, he finished well up in the rankings at Intermediate 1. He was still doing just fine.

Kelly was also doing well. Since coming to Southern Pines, she had picked up several new clients and was training and showing horses for other people, including the owner's horse, Winchester, who she took from First

Level to Prix St. George before they were finished. It was her turn to rise – and Andy's turn to rest.

During the winter of that year, Andy continued to train for Grand Prix dressage. He was mastering the extremely demanding movements, but it was getting harder. The strain on the aging gelding's joints was starting to show, and they had to take it a little slower – demand a little less, take care to avoid an injury. Andy was still game, still willing, and every inch a competitor, but it was hard to tell how much longer he could keep up the pace.

Unfortunately, late that winter, Andy did suffer an injury to his stifle (hind knee). No one knew exactly what happened, but it was suspected that he may have slipped or fallen in his pasture. It was a serious injury and Andy spent the next two months confined to a stall, slow hand walking his only form of exercise. The injury healed, but Andy was never quite the same, never fully sound again.

Further X-rays and investigation found the beginning of fusion in Andy's hock joints. Kelly had to make some serious decisions. She could have him operated on to fuse the joints all the way. This would reduce his discomfort and make him ridable again, but it was a very painful surgery and recovery for the horse to endure. Or, she could let Mother Nature do the job over time. That would mean retiring the big horse for good.

Kelly was disappointed. He had been training so well at Grand Prix Level. The wild black mustang had made it all the way to the top. But she was proud of him, too, and she knew what she had to do. Not wanting to cause him any more pain, and knowing he had more than earned his retirement, Kelly turned him out to pasture with a group of yearlings. He was back to the job he loved best of all. As a babysitter to the youngest horses, he was, and always would be, at the top of the pecking order.

9

Retired Horse

For the next year, Andy enjoyed the freedom of the pasture and the undisturbed routine of herd life in a way that he had not done since his own colthood on the Nevada range and the BLM ranches. He dozed in the morning sun, ate at his leisure, always tolerant of the playful colts and fillies he chaperoned each day. Slowly, the discomfort left his legs, and he was often seen frisking with the babies like a youngster again. Kelly visited him often, and he was always glad to see her, nickering his greeting, reveling in the attention she gave him, and as always, seeking treats.

Kelly and Andy were happy and settled, enjoying a good spell in their lives, but Southern Pines would close its doors to the public in 2001, leaving them looking for a new home once again.

In July, they moved to Cabin Gulch Stables, in Elizabeth, Colorado. It was another large show stable where there was plenty of work for Kelly and weanlings to watch over for Andy. The transition was a positive one for them and they were soon a part of the friendly, supportive "family" of the stable.

Mother Nature had done her job over the past year, fusing Andy's hock joints completely and making him comfortable again. Kelly start to ride him, lightly and just for fun now. Andy seemed happy to have her back. He loved the leisurely trail rides that gave him a break from his pasture and time with his favorite person.

It was nice for Kelly, too. Time spent with Andy was time away from clients and training and competitive pressures, time away from financial worries and marriage concerns. As she had learned early on, she put all of that aside when she went to Andy. Everything disappeared except the two of them. He was good therapy for her, and she needed him now more than ever.

An official retirement ceremony took place at a show in High Prairie that summer. For the last time, Andy was shipped to the show site and settled into a stall to await his moment in the spotlight. Kelly, and her long-time groom, Paula Peterson, attended to the old horse just as carefully as if they were about to enter the most important class of their lives – polishing the enormous hooves, braiding the thick mane, wrapping the lower legs in immaculate white wraps, and brushing the dark coat until it gleamed.

Although he lacked the muscle tone of his earlier days, Andy looked just as majestic and elegant as he ever had, and if he was feeling any discomfort in his tired legs, he didn't show it, as Kelly rode him into the arena.

The show announcer told Andy's remarkable tale as the great black horse trotted and cantered around the ring. Kelly made no demands on him, but he arched his neck proudly and moved in his old, powerful way. The announcer recalled for the hushed crowd Andy's wild beginnings, his prison training, his years with Ginger Scott, and his rise to the upper levels of the dressage world and as a mustang representative with Kelly.

Then, Kelly and JB Andrew moved to the center of the arena and halted, saluting the spectators for the last time. Music played softly all around them. Kelly patted the horse's damp neck and dismounted. Andy's saddle was removed – the official sign of a horse's retirement – and

Paula quickly wiped the sweat off the black coat while Kelly stood at his head, speaking quiet words to him.

A wreath of pure white flowers was draped over Andy's neck. Kelly's freckled face sparkled with tears as she smiled up at him.

All of the people who had made his special life possible were publicly thanked, and those who were there entered the arena to stand next to the distinguished old gelding. Kelly's husband, Dave, her mother, Ginger Scott (Ginger was not able to attend), two veterinarians, several farriers, Sue Halasz, Paula Peterson, Peter Stone and Sherry Bell (representing the BLM), were all offered sincere thanks. Sherry Bell presented Kelly with a plaque for Andy that read "May You Continue to be the Most Famous Mustang in America."

The announcer offered wishes, on behalf of Andy's supporters and fans, that he enjoy his new life of leisure at Cabin Gulch, and invited the public to join Andy and his crew for ice cream at the stables.

The applause was loud and long as JB Andrew was led from the ring, and there were many tears amongst the smiles.

In 2002, Andy was inducted into the Wild Horse and Burro Hall of Fame, as the first, and only, mustang to reach the FEI levels of the elite dressage world. Since

then, several other mustangs have competed success-fully in dressage, although none have yet matched his record. Andy did well in the dressage ring, but he did even more to pave the way for people to dream and believe, and to try and succeed, with a breed never before thought to be capable of competitive dressage. In many ways, JB Andrew made his mark on the world.

Andy lived an easy life for the next few years, babysitting and enjoying his retirement. Kelly used him as a lesson horse at times, but she had a hard time sharing her friend with clients. It was hard to watch as an inexperienced rider struggled to get him to do basic movements when she knew the intricate, powerful actions he had been capable of not so long ago.

Kelly took a new job at Harmony Stables in 2005, and, as always, Andy moved with her. It would be one of the toughest years they would ever endure together.

Harmony Stables was built on a site where an Indian massacre had supposedly taken place long, long ago. Many people believed that the area was cursed and full of "negative energy." It wasn't long before Kelly started to wonder if they were right.

Andy seemed unhappy there, sullen and uncoopera-tive in a way Kelly had never known him to be. The horse who had managed to stay reasonably sound for the past few years gradually became sore again, and soon could barely be ridden. The stable even had a "voodoo pasture," where it was said that any pregnant mare that had been put there had lost her foal.

Kelly's marriage ended that year, and her client load slipped drastically. It was, by all standards, one of the lowest years the pair had experienced together. In April, 2006, they moved back to Cabin Gulch.

Andy lives there now, a happy, contented horse once more. He is no longer sore and is back to his jobs of babysitting weanlings and yearlings, occasionally teaching new riders, and being one of Kelly's best friends. He is becoming a bit more obstinent in his old age, and his eyes are beginning to fail a little, but he still greets Kelly at the fence with a whinny, still hunts eagerly for the treats she always brings him, and he still guards her from the other horses, demanding that any attention she has to give goes to him alone.

In the wild, Andy would likely not have lived to see such an easy old age. In a way, he is freer now than he ever was as a colt in the mountains of Nevada.

I O

Full Circle

Ginger Scott moved to Worthington, Massachusetts, in the summer of 2006, and bought herself a small farm. When she speaks of Andy, her voice is full of pride, but also a sadness that remains after all these years, a regret about having to sell her mustang. She still loves him dearly. Although she stopped visiting him after he and Kelly moved to Southern Pines, she continued to keep in touch with Kelly, and the two women remain friends.

There is a possibility that Andy may return to Ginger and live out his old age on her farm, with a pasture of his own and the company of a herd of Percherons in an adjoining field.

For Ginger, this would be the perfect ending, a chance to share, once more, in the horse of her dreams. Kelly, busy now with a new horse, Opus, an abundance of clients, and keeping up the first house of her own, hasn't yet decided if she's able to let him go, but she is considering it. She worries about the trailer ride – she notices the strain on his joints when he travels now, even for short distances. She knows she would miss him incredibly. But she also realizes that it would be the perfect place for an old, wild horse to live out his days, loved and well cared for to the end – and a beautiful gift for Ginger.

For Ginger, Kelly, and JB Andrew, life has come full circle, with friends coming together, drifting apart, and returning again through trials and successes, good times and hard times, but always bound by the love of a magnificent, big, black horse.

About the Author

Judy Andrekson grew up in Nova Scotia with a pen in one hand and a lead rope in the other. At the age of twenty, she moved to Alberta, where she could pursue her great love of horses, and there she worked for six years, managing a thoroughbred racehorse farm. By her thirties, Judy had also begun to write seriously. Now she combines both of her passions in her new series for young readers, True HORSE Stories. Judy also works as an educational assistant. She, her husband, and their daughter live in Sherwood Park, Alberta, with a constantly changing assortment of animals.

True HORSE Stories by Judy Andrekson:

Little Squire: The Jumping Pony
Miskeen: The Dancing Horse
JB Andrew: Mustang Magic
Fosta: Marathon Master

Praise for True Horse Stories

"Sherwood Park author Judy Andrekson's characters dance, prance and bow in this new series of children's books called True Horse Stories.

Andrekson clearly understands and loves horses . . . . What makes these books unique in the large "horse genre" of literature is that the stories are based on actual, non-fictional accounts of horses from around the world."
— *Strathcona County This Week*

"Short and easy to read, but with lots of impact, these two books are highly recommended."
— *Resource Links (rating: Excellent)*

Praise for *Little Squire: The Jumping Pony*

"*Little Squire* is a true story based on the recollections of friends and family of Mickey Walsh. Author Judy Andrekson's love of horses rings clear and true. The illustrations by David Parkins imbue a sense of joy which is seen in the faces of both humans and horse. This is a lovely book, and I would recommend it not only to horse lovers, but to young readers who enjoy historical fiction. **Highly Recommended.**"
— *Manitoba Library Association*

Praise for *Miskeen: The Dancing Horse*

". . . *Miskeen* was my favourite because the story is so sad . . . . Andrekson describes a beautiful picture of an old, mistreated horse. Alone in a field it dances and bows to an invisible audience."   – *The St. Albert Gazette*

". . . it was *Miskeen: The Dancing Horse* that really sent me galloping back to the wholly imaginary paddock of my childhood . . . . In this book Andrekson really embraces the storytelling heart of her material."
                                   – *Quill & Quire* (Feature Review)